TELL ME
ABOUT
PIONEERS

Acknowledgements

For permission to reproduce copyright material, the author and publishers gratefully acknowledge the following;

cover National Library of Jamaica **back cover** National Library of Jamaica **title page** National Library of Jamaica **page 5** National Library of Jamaica **page 6** Travel Ink **page 7** Mary Evans Picture Library **page 8** (top) Mary Evans Picture Library (bottom) National Library of Jamaica **page 9** Robert Harding Picture Library **page 10** Bridgeman Art Library/City of Bristol Museum and Art Gallery, Avon/Private Collection **page 11** Bridgeman Art Library **page 12** Bridgeman Art Library/Private Collection **page 13** Mary Evans Picture Library **page 14** Bridgeman Art Library/Victoria & Albert Museum, London **page 15** (top) Courtesy of the Director, National Army Museum, London (middle) National Library of Jamaica **page 16** Bridgeman Art Library/Greater London Council **page 17** Mary Evans Picture Library **page 18** The Illustrated London News Picture Library **page 19** Bodleian Library, University of Oxford. (shelfmark 249 t 548) **page 20** Sascha Rooij **page 21** By courtesy of the National Portrait Gallery, London

TELL ME ABOUT PIONEERS

MARY SEACOLE

written by
John Malam

Evans

Evans Brothers Limited

Contact the Author

Tell me what you think about this book.
Write to me at Evans Brothers.
Or e-mail me at: johnmalam@aol.com

First published in paperback
in 2005 by Evans Brothers Limited
2A Portman Mansions
Chiltern St London W1U 6NR

© Evans Brothers Limited 1999

First published 1999
Reprinted 2001, 2003
Printed in China by WKT Company Limited

British Library Cataloguing in Publication data.

Malam, John
   Mary Seacole
   1. Seacole, Mary, 1805-1881 - Juvenile literature 2. Crimean
   War, 1853-1856 - Women - Juvenile literature
   I. Title
   610.7'3'092

ISBN 0237528177

VISIT OUR WEBSITE
www.evansbooks.co.uk
Evans

When Mary's mother was young, she had been taken against her will to Jamaica, from her home in Africa. On Jamaica she was a slave, like thousands of other black people. They were made to work very hard and were not free people. Mary's mother was lucky because after a while she was given her freedom back.

Slaves on Jamaica worked in the sugar cane fields. Slavery went on there until it was stopped in 1838.

Mary and her family lived in the busy port of Kingston, the capital of Jamaica.

Mary's mother's house looked like this one.

Mary's family was quite well off. Her mother owned a large house with lots of rooms. People paid money to stay there when they were ill. Mary's mother looked after them. People called her a 'doctress' because she healed the sick.

Mary's mother made medicines from plants. She knew about them from her old home in Africa. Mary helped her, and learned a lot of useful things.

We do not know if Mary went to school. We do know that she played at being a nurse. She pretended that her pets were ill. She gave them medicine and put bandages on their legs!

Jamaica is hot and wet. Lots of plants grow there.

As a child, Mary heard stories about faraway places, told by soldiers and sailors who came to Kingston. She wanted to visit them.

When she was twelve, Mary went to England. She went across the sea on a big ship. It landed at Bristol, and from there Mary travelled by coach to London. In London, she met her father's family for the first time. Mary stayed in England for nearly a year.

This is what Bristol harbour looked like when Mary arrived there by ship in 1817.

England was not at all like Jamaica. Because there were not many black people, Mary looked different. Some people pointed at her, and called her unkind names because of the colour of her skin. When she was older, Mary wrote about how children had made fun of her.

London was a much bigger city than Kingston. To Mary it seemed cold, grey and smoky.

Mary visited the islands of Cuba, Haiti and the Bahamas.

After a year, Mary went back home to Jamaica, where she began to make jams and pickles to sell. She used the money to pay for trips to other islands in the West Indies. Travel by ship was uncomfortable, and sometimes it was dangerous. One ship Mary was on caught fire!

Mary learned about the plants healers used in all the places she went to. She learned to be a doctress, just like her mother.

When Mary was thirty-one she married Edwin Horatio Seacole. Now her name was Mrs Seacole. But her new husband died soon after.

Mary worked harder than ever. She made medicines which cured people who were sick with yellow fever and cholera. Both diseases could kill people – but Mary's medicines saved them.

In 1850 Mary went to Panama, a country in Central America, to visit her brother Edward. She worked there as a nurse and healer.

This picture shows people on horseback crossing a river in Panama. Mary must have travelled like this too.

Mary heard about a war in Europe. Britain, France and Turkey fought against Russia, in an area called the Crimea. The war was the Crimean War.

Lots of Mary's soldier friends were sent to fight in the war. Many were hurt, and Mary wanted to nurse them.

She went to London, hoping she would be sent to the Crimea to work as a nurse. But she was told she could not go.

Photographs and paintings showed people at home how terrible the Crimean War was. Many soldiers were killed.

Mary called her canteen the British Hotel. It was a wooden hut. It is on the left of the top picture.

Mary's hut was also a shop. Mary is the lady in the hat.

Mary went anyway, using her own money to pay for the long journey. She set sail in January 1855, and arrived in the Crimea in the summer.

Mary took lots of useful things with her. She set up a canteen and store for the soldiers. She fed them and looked after them.

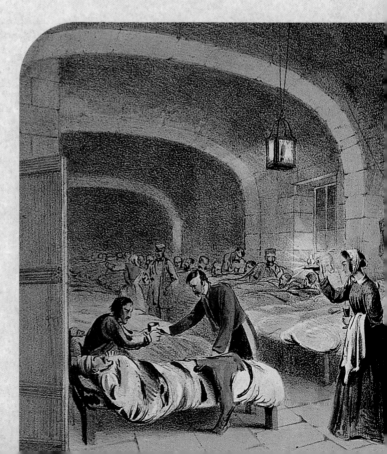

Many soldiers were hurt in the war. There were 'hospitals' in tents, but they were dirty places. A famous nurse called Florence Nightingale worked hard to make the hospitals safer and cleaner.

Mary helped as many soldiers as she could. She even helped them when the fighting was going on all around. She did not worry about being in danger herself.

Florence Nightingale was called 'the lady with the lamp'. Some people called Mary 'the other lady with the lamp'. The two nurses worked through the dark nights, carrying lamps to help them see.

Mary gave the soldiers food and medicine, and things to read. Most of all she gave them love and care.

A newspaper writer said: "She is always on the battlefields. A more skilful hand about a wound or a broken limb could not be found." The newspaper was 'The Times', a very important paper. By reading this paper, people all over Britain learned about Mary Seacole.

Mary called the soldiers 'her sons'. They called her 'Mother Seacole'. They were always pleased to see her.

This picture shows the end of the Crimean War. Mary is in the middle of the line of people, wearing a fine hat with a feather. She is greeting the soldiers as they prepare to leave for home.

After the war, Mary went to London. She was given medals as a way of thanking her for taking care of the wounded soldiers.

Mary had no money left. But she had lots of new friends. They held a music show to help her, which 40,000 people went to. 'The Times' newspaper said that "the name of Mrs Seacole was shouted by a thousand voices".

Mary wrote a book about her life. It was called 'Wonderful Adventures of Mrs Seacole'. Lots of people read it.

In her book, Mary said that she came back from the war "wounded, as many others did". This meant she felt hurt at seeing how the soldiers had suffered. But she was not sorry she had gone.

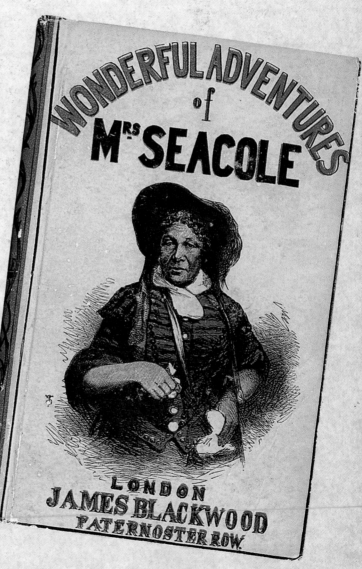

This is the front cover of Mary's book.

Mary spent the rest of her life living between Jamaica and England. She was so famous as a nurse that when the Prince of Wales, Queen Victoria's eldest son, was ill, it was Mary who made him better.

Mary died in 1881. Even though she was so famous she was soon forgotten. Then, 100 years after her death, nurses from the West Indies and Africa came together to make sure the name of Mary Jane Seacole was known once again. Today, she is remembered as one of the world's most famous nurses.

Mary Seacole was buried in London. This new gravestone was placed on her grave in 1981.

Important dates

1805 Mary Jane Grant was born in Kingston, Jamaica

1817 Age 12 – she visited London for the first time

1836 Age 31 – she married Edwin Horatio Seacole

1843 Age 38 – her house in Kingston burnt down

1850 Age 45 – she went to Panama, in Central America

1854 The Crimean War started in Europe

1855 Age 50 – she went by ship to the Crimea

1856 The Crimean War ended. Mary went back to London

1857 Age 52 – she wrote her book. It was called 'Wonderful Adventures of Mrs Seacole'

1881 Age 76 – she died and was buried in London

This model of Mary was made in 1871, when she was an old lady. She is wearing her medals.

Keywords

doctress
a female doctor

healer
a person who cures the sick

nurse
someone who looks after
people when they are ill

slave
a person who is owned by
someone else, and has to
work for them

soldier
someone who fights as part
of an army

Index